Lyrical Solos from the British Isles for

Clarinet and Piano

featuring the "English Sonatina"

James Marshall

Piano Accompaniment

The Cecilio CT-480 clarinet image on the cover is courtesy of Cecilio Musical Instruments.

WWW.MELBAY.COM

Preface

Lyrical Solos from the British Isles is a collection of folk and traditional songs and dances with one hymn and a few original pieces added, all with the aspiring young clarinetist in mind. The author's 2018 "English Sonatina" is prominently featured; this piece was given its repertoire recital premiere in London by clarinetist Alison Eales, demonstrating its suitability for both student recital and professional concert performance.

The modal and folk song-like character of Marshall's "English Sonatina" is reflected in the clarinet and piano arrangements of the other eleven songs in the collection, including such stalwarts as: "The Maiden's Lament", "Emerald Jig", "Wild Mountain Thyme", and "Scarborough Fair" plus two more Marshall originals — "Ballad" and "The Highlands". The folk influence in this music is further enhanced by the innate lyrical quality of the clarinet in combination with complimentary piano accompaniment.

Performance Notes for "English Sonatina"
"English Sonatina" is written in the traditional four-movement structure popular from the Baroque Period to the present. It pays tribute to Ralph Vaughn Williams (*Folk Song Suite*), Benjamin Britten (*Simple Symphony*) and others who incorporated English folk songs in their music. This facet of their work set them apart from the predominantly German school of Bach, Beethoven, Brahms, etc. — establishing a distinctively English school of composition.

Modal and melodic lines characteristic of this style appear in Marshall's sonatina in addition to the more modernist harmonic coloration of Debussy and Vaughn Williams, who often used intervals of a fourth and fifth in addition to triadic harmonies. Changes in quarter-time meters in the opening movement and some polytonality throughout are other more modern facets of this otherwise accessible composition for young students.

The Four Movements:
"Andante cantabile" illustrates the ABA sonata form in that, after a brief introduction, a clearly distinguishable theme is stated and subsequently recapitulated.

The "Scherzo" is set in a lively ¾ meter, again in ABA form.

"Lento" pays homage to Vaughn Williams' fondness for the six-four chord. Here, the reference is notably to the opening of his "Dona Nobis Pacem" [Grant Them Peace].

"Allegro giocoso" states a lively motif that is joined by a quotation of the English folk song, "High Germany" which Vaughn Williams used in "Songs from Somerset" in his *Folk Song Suite.*

Our hope is that these arrangements of well-known tunes together with the author's original compositions and performance notes present an engaging recital repertoire for the young clarinetist.

Index

Ballad

James Marshall

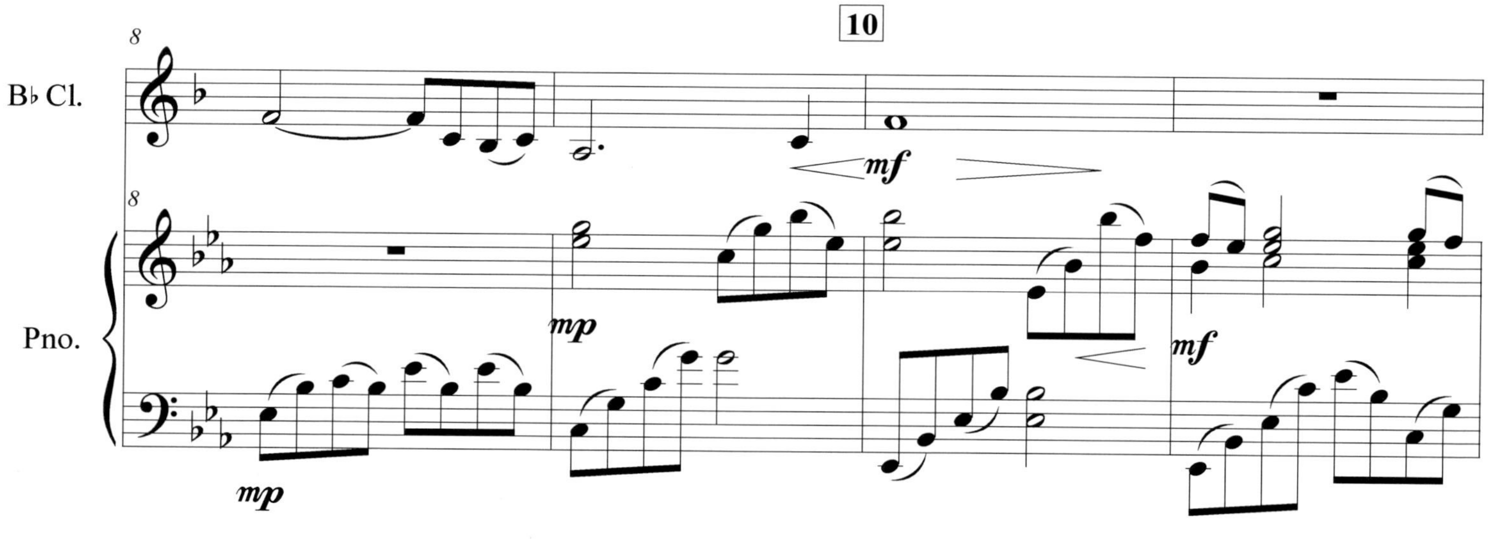
B♭ Cl.
Pno.
10
mf
mp
mf
mp

B♭ Cl.
Pno.
1.
p
mp
mp
p

B♭ Cl.
Pno.
2.

Be Thou My Vision

Irish Christian Hymn
James Marshall

16
B♭ Cl.
mf
Pno.
mf
20
B♭ Cl.
mp
20
Pno.
mp
24
B♭ Cl.
24
Pno.
mp

28
B♭ Cl.
mp
mf
Pno.
mp
32
B♭ Cl.
Pno.
mf
36
B♭ Cl.
f
Pno.
f

44
B♭ Cl.
Pno.

Emerald Jig

Irish Dance
James Marshall

13
B♭ Cl.
Pno.
f
17
1.
21
2.

English Sonatina
For Young Clarinetists

James Marshall

Andante cantabile ♩ = 76

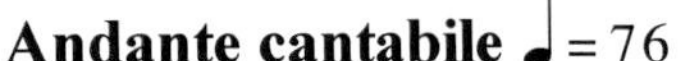

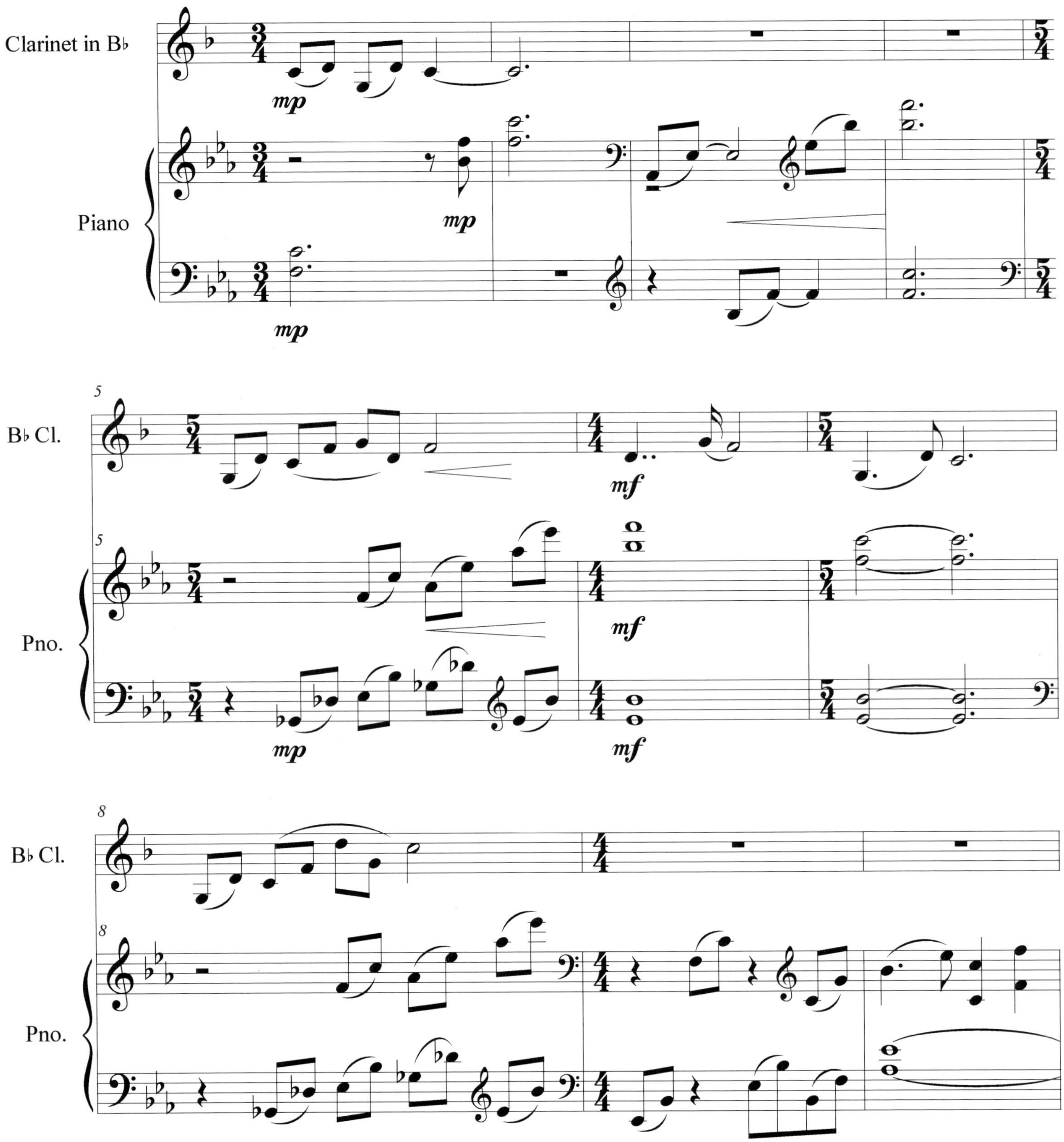

12
B♭ Cl.
Pno.
f
p
mp
B♭ Cl.
Pno.
mp
mf
f
21
B♭ Cl.
Pno.
mp

23
B♭ Cl.
23
Pno.
27
B♭ Cl.
27
Pno.
31
B♭ Cl.
mf
p
mf
31
Pno.
mf
p
mf
mf
p
mf

B♭ Cl.
Pno.
mp
f
p
mf
43

B♭ Cl.
Pno.
rit.

Scherzando ♩= 142
Bb Cl.
Pno.
f
66
mf
mp
cresc.
1.

75
2.
77
B♭ Cl.
f
mp
Pno.
82
87
D.S. al Coda

Coda
B♭ Cl.
Pno.
p
cresc.
f
Lento ♩ = 66
mp

106
B♭ Cl.
mp
106
Pno.
mp
mp
111
B♭ Cl.
mf
111
Pno.
mf
mf
117
115
B♭ Cl.
mp
115
Pno.
mp

119
B♭ Cl.
mf
Pno.
mf
Allegro giocoso ♩ = 82
122
B♭ Cl.
f
Pno.
f
f
126
B♭ Cl.
mf
Pno.
mf

130
B♭ Cl.
Pno.
mf
mp
134
mf
mp
p
137
139
cresc.

143
B♭ Cl.
mp
143
mp
Pno.
mp
147
B♭ Cl.
147
Pno.
rit.
152
"High Germany" Folk Song
151
B♭ Cl.
f
151
Pno.
f
f

155
B♭ Cl.
mf
Pno.
mp
mp
162
159
B♭ Cl.
Pno.
163
B♭ Cl.
Pno.

170
B♭ Cl.
Pno.
mf
mp
f

181
179
B♭ Cl.
mf
179
Pno.
mf
183
B♭ Cl.
183
Pno.
189
187
B♭ Cl.
187
Pno.

191
B♭ Cl.
191
Pno.
194
B♭ Cl.
mp
194
Pno.
mp
mp
197
B♭ Cl.
mf
197
Pno.
mf
mf

200
B♭ Cl.
subito p
Pno.
mp
mp
203
f
f
f
206

Lyrical Solos from the British Isles for

Clarinet and Piano

featuring the "English Sonatina"

James Marshall

Clarinet Solo Part

WWW.MELBAY.COM

Preface

Lyrical Solos from the British Isles is a collection of folk and traditional songs and dances with one hymn and a few original pieces added, all with the aspiring young clarinetist in mind. The author's 2018 "English Sonatina" is prominently featured; this piece was given its repertoire recital premiere in London by clarinetist Alison Eales, demonstrating its suitability for both student recital and professional concert performance.

The modal and folk song-like character of Marshall's "English Sonatina" is reflected in the clarinet and piano arrangements of the other eleven songs in the collection, including such stalwarts as: "The Maiden's Lament", "Emerald Jig", "Wild Mountain Thyme", and "Scarborough Fair" plus two more Marshall originals — "Ballad" and "The Highlands". The folk influence in this music is further enhanced by the innate lyrical quality of the clarinet in combination with complimentary piano accompaniment.

Performance Notes for "English Sonatina"

"English Sonatina" is written in the traditional four-movement structure popular from the Baroque Period to the present. It pays tribute to Ralph Vaughn Williams (*Folk Song Suite*), Benjamin Britten (*Simple Symphony*) and others who incorporated English folk songs in their music. This facet of their work set them apart from the predominantly German school of Bach, Beethoven, Brahms, etc. — establishing a distinctively English school of composition.

Modal and melodic lines characteristic of this style appear in Marshall's sonatina in addition to the more modernist harmonic coloration of Debussy and Vaughn Williams, who often used intervals of a fourth and fifth in addition to triadic harmonies. Changes in quarter-time meters in the opening movement and some polytonality throughout are other more modern facets of this otherwise accessible composition for young students.

The Four Movements:

"Andante cantabile" illustrates the ABA sonata form in that, after a brief introduction, a clearly distinguishable theme is stated and subsequently recapitulated.

The "Scherzo" is set in a lively ¾ meter, again in ABA form.

"Lento" pays homage to Vaughn Williams' fondness for the six-four chord. Here, the reference is notably to the opening of his "Dona Nobis Pacem" [Grant Them Peace].

"Allegro giocoso" states a lively motif that is joined by a quotation of the English folk song, "High Germany" which Vaughn Williams used in "Songs from Somerset" in his *Folk Song Suite.*

Our hope is that these arrangements of well-known tunes together with the author's original compositions and performance notes present an engaging recital repertoire for the young clarinetist.

Index

Ballad

James Marshall

Emerald Jig

Irish Dance
James Marshall

Be Thou My Vision

Irish Christian Hymn
James Marshall

Singing, heralding ♩ = 88

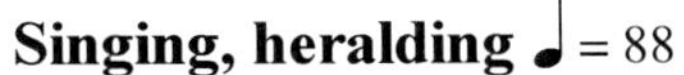

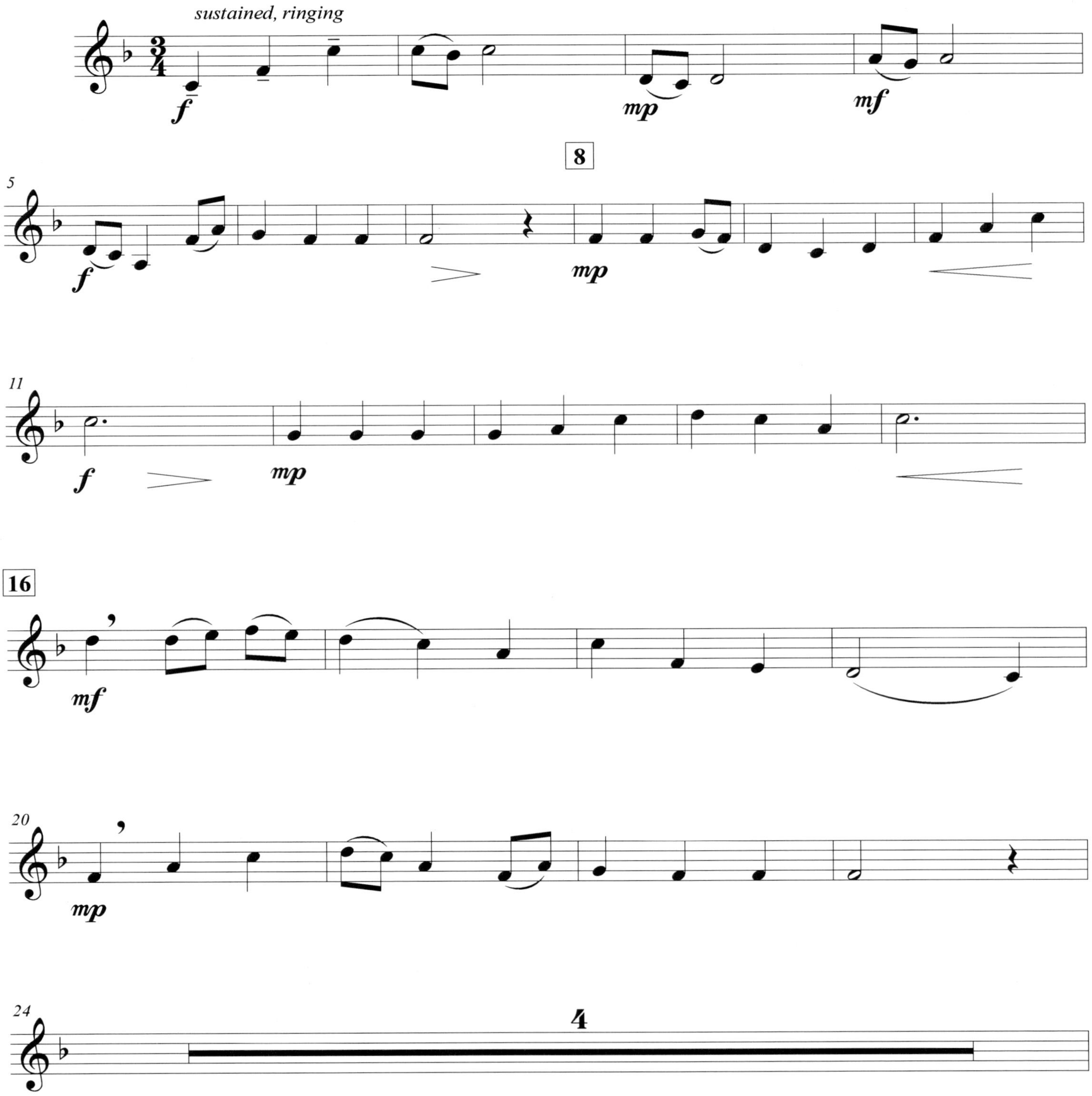

28
mp
mf
32
36
f
40
p
mf
44
4
48
mf
52
mp

English Sonatina
For Young Clarinetists

James Marshall

36
mp
5
4
4
4
41
43
f
44
p
mf
47
mf
mp
50
mp
53
55
mf
5
4
56
5
4
mp
4
4
Scherzando ♩ = 142
59
3
4
7

66
mf
mp
cresc.
mf
73
1.
2.
mf
f
77
mp
79
2
85
87
D.S. al Coda
3
Coda
93
p
cresc.
f
98
Lento ♩ = 66
p
104
106
mp
mp
111
mf
mp
117
mf

Allegro giocoso ♩ = 82
122
Pa
f
126
mf
131
mp
mf
136
137
mp
p
cresc.
141
mp
146
151
rit.
152
"High Germany" Folk Song
f
156
mf
161
162

170
166
mf
171
mp
176
mf
f
mf
181
189
186
191
196
mp
mf
200
subito p
f
204

How Many Miles to London Town?

Traditional English Song
James Marshall

Flow Gently, Sweet Afton

Jonathan E. Spilman
James Marshall

mp
mp
3
33
mf
p
cadenza
mf
42
3
mp

Scarborough Fair

English Folk Song
James Marshall

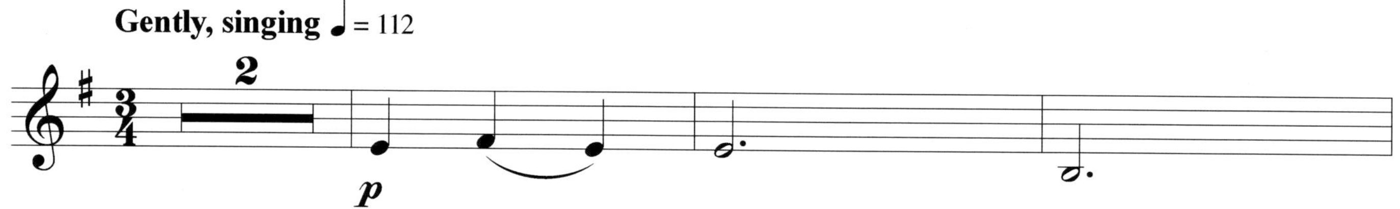

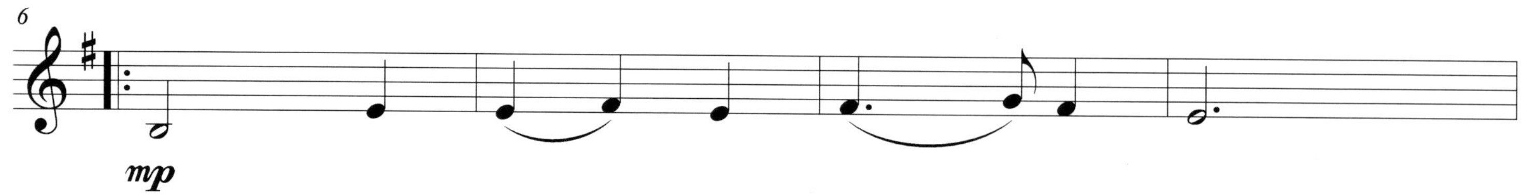

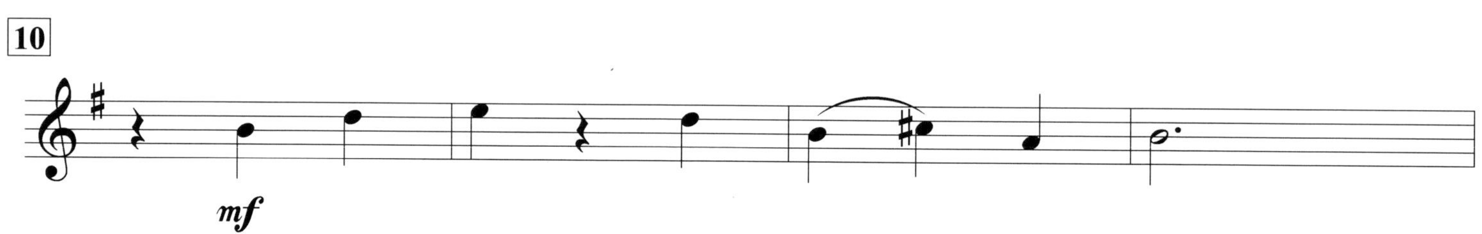

22
mp
mf
28
33
mp
34
38
2
p
42
1.
2.
45
mf
p

The Highlands

James Marshall

54
mf
57
60
f
63
66
p
mp
69
p
75
78
mp
p
81
mp
mf
f
87
mp
91
p

The Girl I Left Behind Me

English Folk Song
James Marshall

The Maiden's Lament

English Folk Song
James Marshall

Time Stands Still

John Dowland
James Marshall

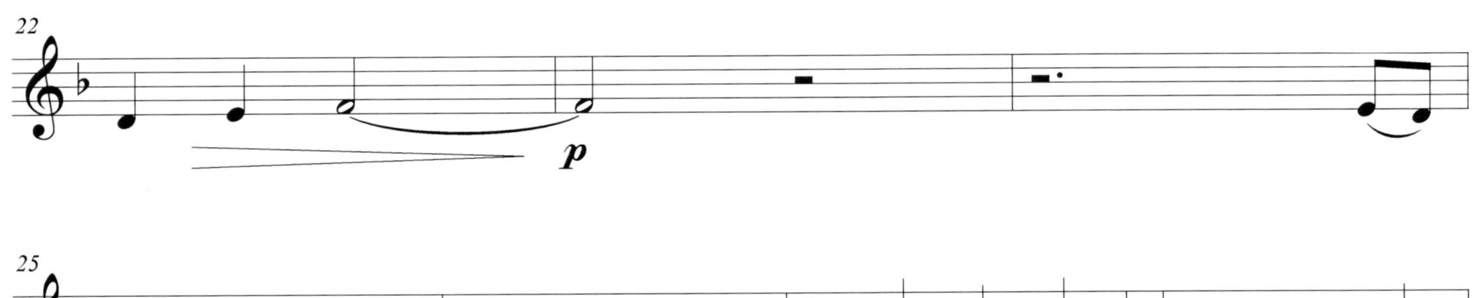
22
p

25
mp
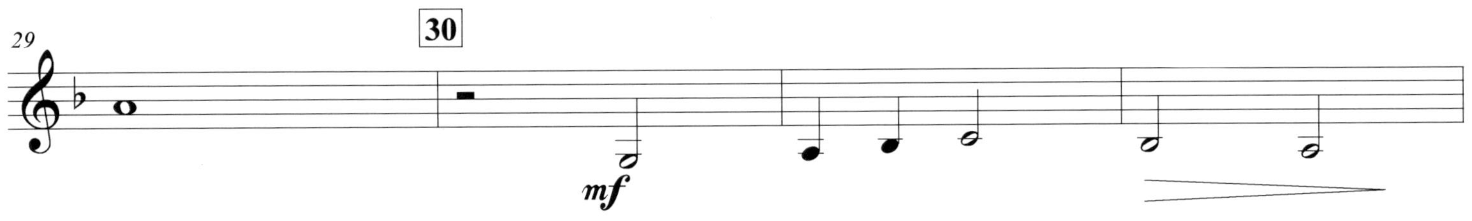
29
30
mf
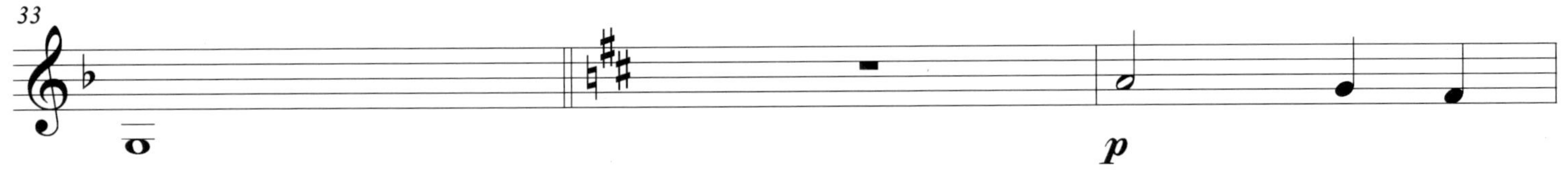
33
p
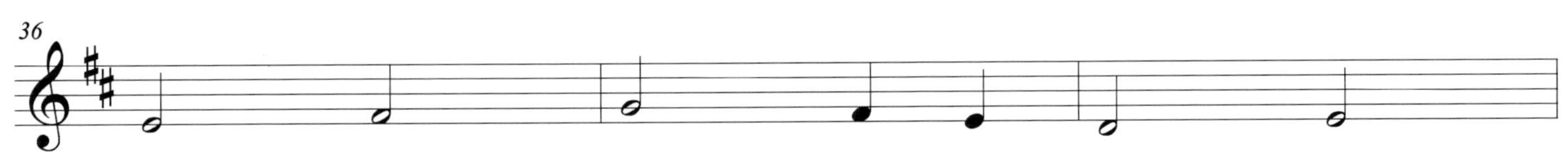
36

rit.
39

Wild Mountain Thyme

Scottish Folk Song
James Marshall

How Many Miles to London Town?

Traditional English Song
James Marshall

B♭ Cl.
Pno.
mf
21
mp

29
B♭ Cl.
Pno.
mf
1.
2.
36
mp
f

Flow Gently, Sweet Afton

Jonathan E. Spilman
James Marshall

13
B♭ Cl.
mf
13
Pno.
mf
17
21
B♭ Cl.
p
17
Pno.
p
23
B♭ Cl.
mp
mp
23
Pno.
mp
mp

27
B♭ Cl.
Pno.
mp
mp
33
32
mf
p
mf
p
37
mf
mf

cadenza
41
B♭ Cl.
Pno.
42
46
mp

Scarborough Fair

English Folk Song
James Marshall

17
21
B♭ Cl.
Pno.
mp
p
f
23
mf
29
33

35
B♭ Cl.
p
35
p
Pno.
p
41
B♭ Cl.
1.
2.
41
Pno.
45
B♭ Cl.
mf
p
45
Pno.
mf
mp
p

The Girl I Left Behind Me

English Folk Song
James Marshall

12
B♭ Cl.
12
Pno.
p
16
B♭ Cl.
mp
mf
16
Pno.
mp
mf
20
B♭ Cl.
20
Pno.

Fine
25
B♭ Cl.
Pno.
D.S. al Fine

The Highlands

James Marshall

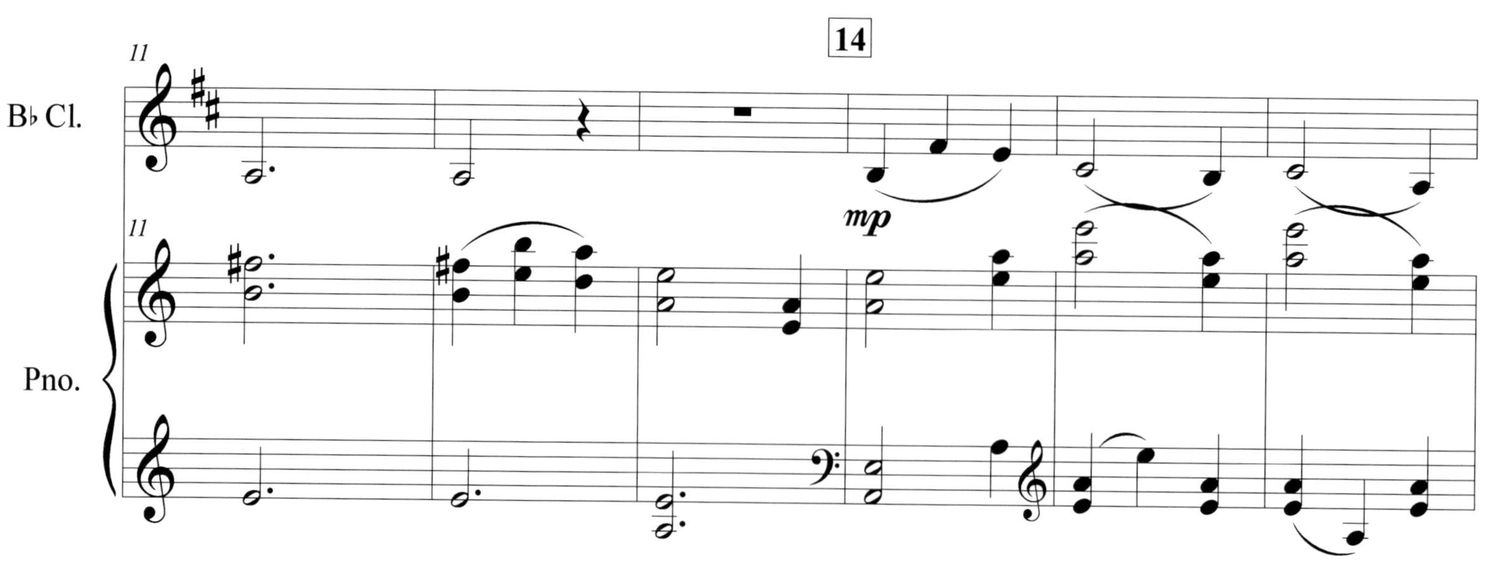

17
B♭ Cl.
Pno.
26
23
mf
mp
29

B♭ Cl.
Pno.
40
mf
mp
B♭ Cl.
Pno.
mp
mp
B♭ Cl.
Pno.
mp

54
53
B♭ Cl.
mf
53
Pno.
mp
57
B♭ Cl.
57
Pno.
61
B♭ Cl.
f
61
Pno.
mf

66
B♭ Cl.
Pno.
78

81
B♭ Cl.
mp
mf
f
81
Pno.
mp
mf
f
mp
87
B♭ Cl.
mp
87
Pno.
mp
91
B♭ Cl.
p
91
Pno.
p

Wild Mountain Thyme

Scottish Folk Song
James Marshall

8
B♭ Cl.
Pno.
mf
mp
11
1.
14
2.

The Maiden's Lament

English Folk Song
James Marshall

B♭ Cl.
Pno.
20
mf
p
mf

B♭ Cl.
Pno.
mp
p
mp
30
1.
2.

Time Stands Still

John Dowland
James Marshall

15
13
B♭ Cl.
mf
p
mp
f
13
mf
p
mp
f
Pno.
21
18
B♭ Cl.
mp
f
18
mp
f
p
Pno.
mp
p
23
B♭ Cl.
p
mp
23
p
mp
Pno.

30
28
B♭ Cl.
Pno.
mf
mf
mp
33
p
p
38
rit.

Other Recommended Mel Bay Clarinet Books

100 Essential Exercises for Clarinet (Elliott)
American Song Collection for Clarinet and Piano (Marshall)
Tone and Technique Studies for the Novice Clarinetist (Marshall)
Modern Etudes for Low Clarinet (Marshall)
Clarinet Fingering Chart (W. Bay)
Clarinet Fingering and Scale Chart (Nelson)
Complete Jazz Clarinet Book (W. Bay)
Technical Development for the Clarinetist (Heim)
Tone, Technique & Staccato (Galper)
Upbeat Scales & Arpeggios (Galper)
Clarinet Solos on Balkan Folk Songs and Dances (Puscoiu)
Easy Klezmer Tunes (Phillips)
Klezmer Book (Galper)
20 Clarinet Duets from Baroque to the 20th Century (Heim)
25 Solos for Clarinet(Bach/Leonard)
Baroque Music for Clarinet (Heim)
Classical Repertoire for Clarinet Volume One (Puscoiu)
Favorite Student Clarinet Classics (W. Bay)
International and Classic Favorites for Clarinet Solo (Heim)
Laurindo Almeida: Duets for Clarinet and Guitar (Purcell)
Mozart for Clarinet (Heim)
Music of Brahms for Clarinet (Heim)
Recital Pieces for Clarinet from the Period of Impressionism (Heim)
My Very Best Christmas: Trumpet, Clarinet, Soprano Sax (Khanagov)
Solo Pieces for the Beginning Clarinetist (Heim)
Solo Pieces for the Intermediate Clarinetist (Heim)
Solo Pieces for the Advanced Clarinetist (Heim)
101 Easy Songs for Clarinet (Maroni)
Beginning Clarinetist's Songbook (Maroni)
Easy Classics for Clarinet with Piano Accompaniment (Spitzer)
Easy Duets for Clarinet (Puscoiu)
Fun with the Clarinet (W. Bay)
More Fun with the Clarinet (W. Bay)
Solo Pieces for the Beginning Clarinetist (Heim)
Christmas Solos for Beginning Clarinet Level 1 (Heim)
Instrumental Caroling Book (W. Bay)
Sacred Melodies for Clarinet Solo (Heim)